MW01355404

To:_____

From:_____

Please place your photo here.

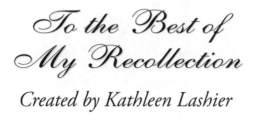

To the Best of My Recollection

Created by Kathleen Lashier

Copyright © 1992, 2006, Linkages

To contact the author:

Linkages Memory Journals • P.O. Box 8282 • Des Moines, IA 50301
888-815-9063
www.mymemoryjournals.com

Printed in the U.S.A.
by G&R Publishing Co.

ISBN-13: 978-1-56383-060-0
ISBN-10: 1-56383-060-4

Distributed by:

507 Industrial Street • Waverly, IA 50677
800-887-4445 • Fax 800-886-7496

What was your day and date of birth?

January 1

Where were you born?
Be specific.

January 2

Do you know any other circumstances of your birth (who was present, who delivered, etc.)?

January 3

Place a childhood picture in this space.

January 4

Name your brothers and sisters and their years of birth.

January 5

What was your mother's full name?

January 6

What were your mother's date/place and circumstances of birth?

What was your father's full name?

January 8

What were your father's date/place and circumstances of birth?

January 9

What did your father do for a living?

January 10

Did your mother work outside the home?

January 11

Name all the street addresses you can recall and/or all the communities you've lived in and years there.

January 12

January 13

*Tell a nickname your family
gave you and how you got it.*

Tell of any other nicknames in your family.

January 15

Tell a fond memory
of your Grandpa.

January 16

*Tell a fond memory
of your Grandma.*

January 17

Tell about a favorite Aunt.

January 18

Tell about a favorite Uncle.

January 19

Relate an experience or memory of a cousin.

January 20

Did any relatives ever live with you? If not, then relate another memory of cousins, aunts or uncles.

January 21

In what way did your mother usually discipline?

*How did your
father discipline?*

January 23

Tell about the naughtiest thing you ever did.

If you got caught,
describe the consequences.

January 25

Did you ever see a President
or Vice-President in person?

Which of the Presidents in your lifetime
has been your favorite and why?

January 26

Did you ever have an imaginary friend?

January 27

What did you and your brothers or sisters fight about the most?

Tell about an experience or event that drew you together.

January 29

*Tell about the worst winter
storm that you can remember as a child.*

January 30

What did you use to go sledding down a hill in the snow?

January 31

What extras did you use for your snowman's face, buttons, arms, hat, etc.?

February 1

Tell of someone you envied and why.

February 2

Do you remember the first
movie you ever saw
and who starred in it?

February 3

What have been some of
your very favorite movies?

February 4

*How did you first
smash a finger?*

February 5

Who was the most famous person you ever met as a child?

Tell about someone who had a big influence on your life.

February 7

Tell about another influential person in your life.

February 8

Tell about a big lie you told.

February 9

Tell about your first favorite television shows.

February 10

Tell about your very first boyfriend or girlfriend.

February 11

Tell about the Valentine's Day festivities at your school.

February 12

Tell about a special valentine you once gave.

February 13

Tell about a special valentine you once received.

February 14

Tell about your first date.

February 15

Tell about your first kiss.

February 16

What was your
favorite meal as a child?

Tell about family reunions in your childhood.

February 18

*What do you remember as
your favorite subject in school?*

February 19

*What do you remember as
your least favorite school subject?*

February 20

What is the biggest problem you remember having in Grade School?

February 21

What is the biggest problem you remember having in Jr. High school?

February 22

What is the biggest problem you remember having in Sr. High school?

February 23

Tell about a great victory or personal success from your school days.

Did you and your friends ever have a secret hide-out?

February 25

Tell about a favorite restaurant or public place where you and your friends liked to gather.

*Tell about the best pet
you ever had.*

February 27

Tell about other pets you had.

February 28

*Tell about being in a
school play or program.*

March 1

Tell about a school principal you remember.

March 2

Did you ever pretend to be sick as an excuse to stay home from school?

March 3

Did you ever get in trouble for saying a bad word?

March 4

Tell about how you spent your Saturdays during the school years.

March 5

*Tell about how you
spent your Sundays.*

March 6

What was the naughtiest or meanest thing you remember doing in school?

March 7

What were the consequences?

March 8

Tell of a difficult essay or term paper assignment.

March 9

What radio programs or stations were your favorites?

March 10

Tell of a childhood illness.

March 11

Did your parents have a favorite remedy for when you were sick or hurt?

March 12

Did kids ever tease you and why?

March 13

*Do you remember
your first pizza?*

March 14

If you went to college, tell which college you chose and why.

Tell your major and how you chose it.

March 16

Tell me more about your college years, or your work experiences in early adulthood.

March 17

What memories do you have of St. Patrick's Day in your childhood.

March 18

If you ever hitch-hiked, explain.

March 19

*What do you remember as
your favorite time of year? Why?*

March 20

Describe some household chores
you had as a child.

March 21

Describe some outside chores.

March 22

Which chore did you dislike the most and how did you try to get out of it? Did you have a favorite chore?

What bones have you broken and how?

March 24

Did you ever need stitches?

March 25

Do you have any other good stories about being injured?

March 26

Tell about an experience at the doctor's office.

March 27

*Tell about an experience
at the dentist's office.*

March 28

Name your best school friends.

March 29

Tell of a nickname given to you by friends or classmates. How did you get it? How did you feel about it?

March 30

What were some crazy names
or nicknames in your school?

Do you have a good April Fool's Day story?

April 1

Tell about a practical joke or prank you played on someone.

April 2

Tell about a practical joke or prank someone played on you.

April 3

Did you make your own kites?
Tell about kite-flying in your youth.

April 4

As a child, what did you want to be when you grew up?

What was your best talent?
What other things were you
really good at doing?

April 6

Did you ever bring home or try to adopt a wild animal?

April 7

Make up a limerick about yourself.
There once was a....

April 8

Now make up a limerick about me.
There once was a....

Relate a favorite
spring memory.

April 10

*Did your Mom or Dad
ever find something you had hidden?*

Share a memory of going to church as you were growing up.

April 12

Share a memory about a church social activity.

(If the following Easter topics do not apply, please share your special Holiday memories and traditions.)

Tell about an Easter Egg hunt.

April 14

If your family went to
Easter Sunrise services, tell about it.

April 15

*Tell about any other
Easter tradition.*

April 16

*When you played make-believe,
what did you pretend?*

If you could return to your childhood, what would you do differently?

April 18

*Is there anything you would
do differently as a teenager?*

Did you ever write something that you were really proud of?

April 20

What was the best book you ever read as a youth?

What has been the biggest physical problem you've had to deal with?

April 22

Have you ever
had a superstition?

April 23

Tell about the first time you were ever behind the wheel of a car.

April 24

Where were your best hide-and-seek places?

April 25

Did you ever take anything that wasn't yours?

April 26

What did you do with it?
Did you get caught?

April 27

Do you have a story about a big surprise?

April 28

*What childhood fear
do you remember?*

April 29

Tell about a
May Day tradition.

April 30

What were May Baskets made of and what did they contain?

How much do you remember paying for an ice cream cone?

May 2

Did you have a treehouse?

May 3

Were you ever bitten by a dog?

May 4

Did your Mother ever make a special gift for you?

May 5

Tell a favorite memory
of your mother.

*Tell about some good advice
your mother gave you.*

May 7

Relate your family Mother's Day traditions...or tell me more about the kind of person your mother was.

May 8

*What did you learn
from your mother?*

May 9

Name some popular hit songs from your youth.

May 10

What was your favorite singing group or band?

May 11

Tell about a favorite singer and a song that he/she sang?

What kind of dances did you do as a youth?

May 13

Tell about the first dance you ever went to.

Did your high school have a prom or formal dance?

May 14

Describe your military experience or that of someone in your family.

May 15

*Share some memories involving
a war during your childhood or youth.*

May 16

May 17

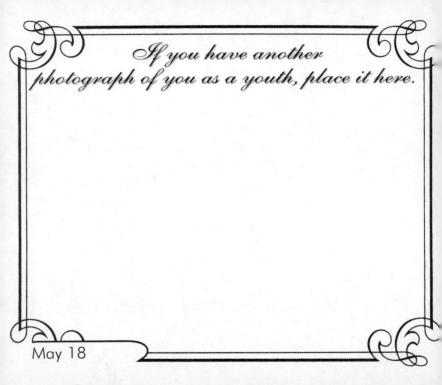

If you have another photograph of you as a youth, place it here.

May 18

*Share some of your
all-time favorites:*

Food –

Books –

May 19

What year did you graduate from high school? What do you recall about your feelings, emotions, hopes and dreams at this time of your life?

May 20

May 21

Tell about your graduation exercises or traditions. How many students were in your graduating class?

May 22

Did you have homework during your school years?

May 23

What was the dumbest stunt pulled by you and a brother or sister?

May 24

Were there consequences?

May 25

*Tell about Memorial Day
traditions during your youth.*

Share a special memory
of Memorial Day.

May 27

*Did you play a
musical instrument?*

May 28

Tell about the closest friend you had in childhood.

May 29

Is there anything you have now that you have kept from your childhood?

Do you have any good bathtime stories?

May 31

Did you have a favorite
nature place you liked to explore?

June 1

*Describe a place you
liked to go to be alone.*

Did you ever sleep under the stars?

June 3

Tell about hot dog or marshmallow roasting.

June 4

Did you ever go on a camp out? Tell about it.

Did you ever go on a snipe hunt?

June 6

Did you have a favorite snack that you made at home?

June 7

Tell about one of the first meals you ever prepared.

Tell about a strange person that lived in your town.

What was your first job?

How much were you paid?

Tell about any other paying jobs you held as a youth.

Were you ever chased by some animal?

June 12

If you were ever in a parade, tell about it.

*Tell another memory
about a parade.*

June 14

Share a childhood memory about a death that affected you.

June 15

Relate your happiest memory as a youth.

June 16

How did you learn to swim?

June 17

Where did you go swimming?

June 18

*Tell a favorite memory
of your father.*

June 19

Tell about some good advice your father gave you.

June 20

Did your father ever make a special gift for you?

June 21

Relate your family Father's Day traditions....or tell me more about the kind of person your father was.

June 22

What did you learn from your father?

June 23

*Did you ever go
skinny-dipping?*

Did you ever make mud pies?

June 24

Did you ever go barefoot in the summer? If so, relate a painful expereience about stepping on something.

June 25

As a youth, did you do any craft, sewing, stitching or needlework?

Tell about a bike you had.

June 27

Tell about your first very own car.

June 28

Did you ever have or make a swing?

*Tell about seeing something
you thought was very beautiful.*

June 30

*Describe an outside game
you made up.*

*Describe an inside game
you made up.*

July 2

What kind of fireworks did people have when you were a youth?

July 3

Tell about Independence Day traditions of your childhood.

July 4

*Do you have a special
July 4th that you remember most?*

July 5

Did you ever go to carnivals or amusement parks? Where?

July 6

What kinds of rides and
games were there?
How much did they cost?

July 7

Tell about any State Fair
or County Fair experiences.

July 8

Tell about going to a circus, a Chautauqua, or a hometown celebration/festival.

July 9

Tell any favorite summertime memory.

July 10

Did you go fishing, hunting or trapping in your youth?

July 11

Tell about your biggest or best catch.

July 12

Do you remember having a favorite candy? How much did it cost?

July 13

Share a horse-riding story.

July 14

Share a memory about going on a picnic.

July 15

*What kinds of party games
or party activities were popular?*

July 16

*Share a memory involving
a heatwave or drought.*

July 17

What did you do to stay cool?

July 18

What was your favorite holiday of the year?

July 19

*Share a birthday
party memory.*

July 20

*Tell about the neatest shoes
you ever owned as a youth.*

*Share a memory about
a power outage.*

July 22

*Relate a memory involving
a flood or cloudburst.*

July 23

*Share a special memory
about riding in a boat.*

July 26

Tell about a family vacation.

July 27

Share the best vacation experience you can recall.

July 28

Share the most unpleasant vacation experience you can recall.

July 29

*Do you have any other
memories about a river,
lake or beach to share?*

Tell a memory about riding on a ferry, bus, train or plane.

*Describe a proud moment
from your childhood.*

August 1

Describe your childhood home.

Describe your neighborhood.

August 3

Tell about your bedroom.

August 4

Tell a memory about having company at your house, or of a family party.

August 5

Tell about board games
you played as a child.

*Tell about card games
you played.*

August 7

Do you have any knowledge of how your first name was chosen?

August 8

Do you have any knowledge
about the origins of your family name?

August 9

Tell about a time when you got lost.

August 10

Did you ever play in the sprinkler or hose?

August 11

Share an experience about
poison ivy, poison weed,
bee strings or bug bites.

Did you have any favorite family songs that you sang together?

August 13

Tell of an experience climbing
a mountain or a big hill.

August 14

Share a memory of staying overnight with a friend.

August 15

If you ever ran away from home, tell about it.

August 16

Do you remember being really curious about something?

Share your childhood experiences with roller skates.

August 18

Did you ever experience home sickness?

Tell about a favorite or least favorite baby-sitter you had.

*Share an early experience
with shaving or make-up.*

Tell about a favorite doll,
teddy bear or other stuffed toy.

August 22

*What other kinds of toys
did you play with?*

August 23

Did you have to abide by a curfew as a youth?

August 24

Describe any "follow the leader" games you played.

Phones have changed over the years. Describe how you used a phone to call up a childhood friend.

Did you ever have a fire in your home or accidentally catch something on fire?

August 27

Tell about going to box socials or pot lucks.

August 28

*Tell about an incident
when you were very angry
with your mom or dad.*

August 29

Tell about an incident when your mom or dad was very angry with you.

Share a memory
involving an outhouse.

August 31

Do you remember any
Labor Day traditions of your youth?

September 1

V J Day...Do you have a
memory involving the end
of World War II?
If not, then share a memory of Vietnam.

September 2

Back-To-School-Days....
What do you rememer about that big
yearly "First Day of School"?

September 3

Tell about your school year calendar.

Tell about a school bully.

September 5

What do you remember doing at recess?

September 6

Tell about the playground equipment at your grade school.

Did your parents ever make you wear something stupid to school?

September 8

Tell about who you thought was the smartest kid in school and why.

September 9

Tell about the naughtiest kid in school.

September 10

How did you experience the 9/11 attacks?

September 11

September 12

Name the schools that you went to.

September 13

What was your most embarrassing school moment?

Name the Grade School teachers you remember.

September 15

Name the Jr. High teachers you remember.

September 16

Name the High School teachers you remember.

September 17

Describe a typical school day outfit in grade school....

In high school....

September 18

Where did you usually buy the clothes you wore?

September 19

If you were ever in a fight,
tell about it.

If you ever had a hero,
tell who and why.

September 21

Tell about a teacher who meant a lot to you and why.

September 22

*Were there any negative
role models who influenced you?*

September 23

How did you get to and from school?

September 24

What were your school colors?

September 25

What was your school mascot?

September 26

Tell any sports you played in Jr. High or High School.

September 27

What was your favorite sport to participate in or watch?

September 28

What other extra-curricular activities did you enjoy?

Do you remember a school custodian?

What is the worst trick that you remember a student playing on a teacher?

What is the meanest thing you ever saw a teacher do to a student?

October 2

Tell about your school lunches.
Did you have a lunch box?
What did you eat?

October 3

Did you ever have a crush on a teacher?

October 4

Do you have any special memories about raking and burning leaves or mowing the lawn?

October 5

If you ever played in the leaves, tell about it.

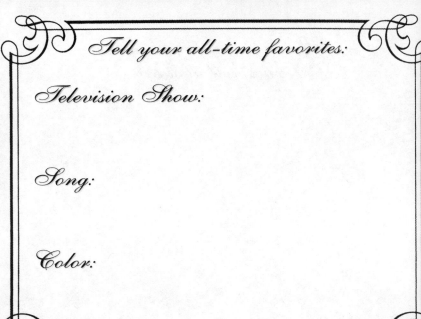

Tell your all-time favorites:

Television Show:

Song:

Color:

October 7

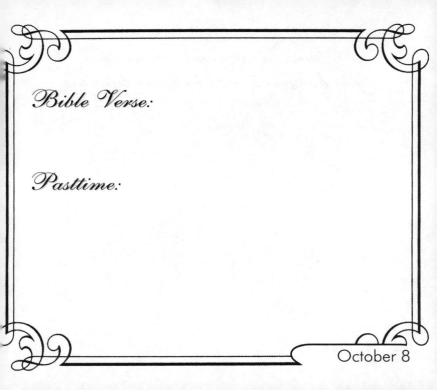

Bible Verse:

Pasttime:

October 8

Share some good advice that __you__ have received in your lifetime.

October 9

October 10

Relate a story about a mouse in the house.

October 11

*Share a memory about
a bat in the house.*

October 12

*What allowance did you get
at different ages during your youth?*

Did you have to do anything to earn it?

October 14

*What have you learned over
the years on how to be wise with money?*

October 15

Tell about pulling or losing a baby tooth.

October 16

Did you ever lose something really important to you?

October 17

Did you ever lose or break something that belonged to someone else?

October 18

Did you ever have a "good friend" who did something mean to you?

October 19

Share a favorite fall memory.

October 20

Did you ever pick apples?

October 21

What is the farthest you ever ran or walked?

October 22

*Did your High School
have cheerleaders? What did they wear?*

October 23

Can you recite any of
the school cheers?

October 24

How did your school observe Homecoming?

October 25

*Do you have any special
Homecoming experiences to relate?*

October 26

Tell about any other
High School extra-curricular activities.

Tell a story about a time when you dressed up in a costume.

October 28

*Share a memory about
being very scared.*

October 29

What did people do at Halloween?

*Do you have a special
Halloween memory?*

October 31

Did you ever tell ghost stories?

November 1

Do you have a good ghost or haunted house story to relate?

November 2

If you have a spouse,
tell how you met.

November 3

What qualities first attracted you to him or her?

November 4

Tell about your wedding day.

November 5

What problems did you have to overcome in the early years of your marriage?

List some things in life
that you are really good at.

November 7

What would you like to learn to do better?

November 8

Who was the President when you were born?

November 9

*When did you cast your first
Presidential vote and for whom?*

November 10

Veteran's Day.....Name the veterans in your family and times during which they served.

November 11

What was your most prized possession as a child?

November 12

*Do you have a story about
standing up against odds for
something you really believed in?*

November 13

Did you ever feel a hatred for another person? Explain.

November 14

Tell about the best birthday present you ever received.

November 15

*Was an injustice
ever done to you?*

November 16

Did you ever make a purchase you later regretted?

November 17

Tell about a memorable birthday cake.

November 18

Have you ever had a recurring dream?

November 19

Describe a few of the favorite hair styles of your youth.

Did you have a watch as a child? What was it like?

Many people remember just what they were doing when they heard of the assassination of John F. Kennedy. If you are not old enough to have that time etched in your memory, relate any other childhood story.

November 22

Share a memory about a
weather-related school cancellation.

November 23

Tell about Thanksgiving traditions of your youth.

What foods were on your
Thanksgiving table?

*Share a favorite
Thanksgiving memory.*

November 26

Do you have any ice skating memories to share?

What hobbies or collections
did you have as a youth?

If you had children, tell their names, dates and places of birth.

November 29

On the next pages, tell some other stories that need to be told.

November 30

December 1

December 2

December 3

December 4

December 5

December 6

Pearl Harbor Day....
If you are not old enough to relate a
memory of that day, relate any other
childhood remembrance.

*Tell abouut your favorite store
to browse in as a youth?
What did you like to look at there?*

What did you first buy using your own money?

December 9

Tell about something you built, designed or made as a youth.

Were you ever in a church or school Christmas or Holiday pageant?

December 11

(If the following Christmas topics do not apply, please share your special Holiday memories and traditions.)

Where did you get your Christmas trees and when did you put them up?

December 12

Tell about how you decorated your Christmas tree.

December 13

Did you hang a Christmas stocking?

December 14

Did your grandma or grandpa ever make gifts for you? What?

December 15

Did your mom or dad ever make gifts for you? What?

December 16

Tell about the best Christmas present you ever received.

December 17

Tell about something special you gave to your mom.

December 18

Tell about something special you gave to your dad.

December 19

Tell about the worst Christmas present you ever received.

December 20

Tell about your experiences with Santa Claus.

December 21

Did you ever go
Christmas caroling?

December 22

Did your family observe the birth of Jesus at Christmas? In what ways?

December 23

*Tell about Holiday
celebrations at a relative's house.*

December 24

Do you remember a
"best" Christmas?

December 25

Share any other Christmas memory.

December 26

Do you remember celebrating any special wedding anniversaries of your parents or grandparents?

December 27

Tell more holiday stories
that need to be told.

December 28

December 29

What special memories do you have of New Year's Eve or New Year's Day?

December 30

If you were to make a
New Year's Resolution this year,
what would it be?

December 31

Memory Journals for Special People

Grandma, Tell Me Your Memories

Grandpa, Tell Me Your Memories

Mom, Share Your Life With Me

Dad, Share Your Life With Me

To the Best of My Recollection

To My Dear Friend

My Days...My Pictures

My Days...My Writings

My Life...My Thoughts

Heirloom Edition – Grandma, Tell Me Your Memories

Heirloom Edition – Mom, Share Your Life With Me

Heirloom Edition – To the Best of My Recollection

Sisters

Mom, Tell Me One More Story...Your Story of Raising Me

Dad, Tell Me One More Story...Your Story of Raising Me